Presented To

_____

_____

By

_____

_____

WHEN TWO BECOME ONE

REFLECTIONS FOR THE NEWLY MARRIED

BY WILLIAM E. HULME

AUGSBURG PUBLISHING HOUSE
Minneapolis, Minnesota

WHEN TWO BECOME ONE

Manufactured in the United States of America

CONTENTS

Preface   7   1719541

Making a Commitment   9

Becoming One Flesh   12

Male and Female He Made Us   15

An Inner Dialog   18

Praying Together   22

An Open Dialog   25

Caring for Feelings   29

Acceptance and Reconciliation   33

Building Up One Another   37

Moving Toward Intimacy   41

"Now Adam Knew His Wife"   45

Sexual Sensitivity   49

Sexual Fulfillment   54

When Two Become Three   58

Parents Are Lovers Too   62

Parents but Still Friends   67

Striking a Balance: Work and Fun   71

The Crossroads of Two Histories   76

Harmony with In-laws   82

Reaching Out to the Community   87

The World Around You   92

PREFACE

When two persons join their lives together the import of the action goes beyond them. Regardless of the particular culture, their action extends to their families, the community in which they live, and the religious group to which they belong. For that reason this book is not only concerned with the various features and dimensions of married life, but also with your relationship to your families, to your community, and to your church.

The purpose of this book is to help you begin and develop an important activity of your life together, that of devotion, meditation, and reflection. In the Christian tradition two familiar features of such reflection are the use of the Bible and of prayer. These remain central in this book. The individual readings lead to the selected Scripture and prepare for the prayer.

The practice of devotion together will help to develop the kind of sharing, honesty, and open communication that are necessary for the continued growth of your relationship. At such times of reflection, tensions can be expressed, misunderstanding clarified, and creative thinking mutually stimulated.

As with any regular activity, the practice of devotion needs its designated time. The usual times are either at the evening meal or at bedtime. Determine which is your best time, then hold to that time as the habit pattern is formed.

The practice of devotion is more than a religious activity separated from other activities of the day. Rather, devotional life is an integrating influence for all daily activities. Devotions together provide that structure for a continual opportunity to reorient ourselves to one another and to the values that are productive for positive living.

But more than values are involved. Religion is also a relationship. As you make it a practice to gather together—the two of you—each day in Christ's name, your relationship with each other is enhanced by the awareness of his presence. The security provided by this awareness is important to the security of your marriage.

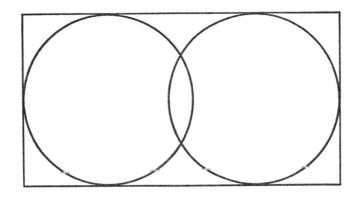

MAKING
A COMMITMENT

Now you are married. You have made a choice and given a promise to live your lives together. Congratulations to the groom and best wishes to the bride.

You made a contract in your marriage service— a commitment. You had made a private commitment before, of course, when you promised to be for one another. On your wedding day, however, you made a public commitment before witnesses. The wedding is like a seal on your relationship. It took place in the presence of people who care about you and whose support you need.

Making a contract of this nature involves a risk. You have declared yourself for the future, and the future is yet to be. Neither of you know what it will be like, and yet you have put yourselves on record concerning what you plan to do with it—together. This takes an element of courage. Small wonder, then, that the act of commitment elicits the finest of human qualities.

Your commitment to one another is one in a long line of tender love stories. One of the most ancient —and touching—is that of Isaac and Rebekah as told in the Old Testament. Isaac's father, Abraham, had sent his servant to the land from which they had come to choose a wife for Isaac. It was common practice in that ancient culture for parents to arrange their children's marriages. To us who appreciate the freedom to initiate our relationship with one another according to our own choice such a practice seems strange.

Yet not all parental choices of mates for their children have proved to be poor choices. Nor have all the choices people have made concerning their own mates proved to be wise choices. In the case of Isaac and Rebekah, parents' and children's choices appear to coincide. For Isaac it was love, if not at first sight, at least in short order. He went to meet the camel caravan bringing his bride. According to the custom of the day she veiled herself. Tenderly he took her into his tent, and, as the Scripture says, "She became his wife, and he loved her."

READ GENESIS 24

In gratitude for the course of events through which we have come to know and to love one another, we ask your continued help, Lord, that, having made our act of commitment to one another, we may have the capacity to fulfill it, through your Son, Jesus Christ our Savior. Amen.

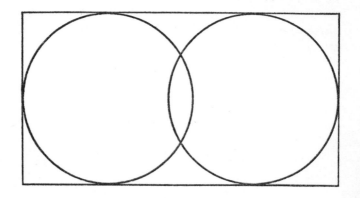

BECOMING
ONE FLESH

"Therefore a man leaves his father and mother and cleaves to his wife, and they become one flesh." These ancient words, still used in marriage ceremonies, stem from the creation account in the book of Genesis. The words "one flesh" describe what it means to be married. As a result of your commitment something new has come into being. You are creating it. Your marriage has an entity of its own. You sense the adventure of bringing it into being. Your marriage is recognized by the community in which you live. You have taken the risk and committed yourselves openly. Now you are one flesh.

The two of you have become one, yet you are separate individuals. You will still need relationships with others apart from your mate. You will need time also for yourself. Yet these times apart from your mate are different from the times when you were alone before you were married. Whether you are alone or spending time with a friend, you do so as one who belongs to another. All your experiences are now related to the reality that you are married. You are one flesh—joined together in spirit even when you are not together physically. This togetherness corresponds to other words from your wedding service: "What therefore God has joined together, let no man put asunder."

Jesus said these words during a conflict with local religious and political leaders about marriage and divorce. In that culture the wife was considered to be the disposable property of the husband. He could divorce her as easily as he could sell his donkey. On the other hand the woman could not divorce her husband. Jesus took a strong stand against this attitude toward divorce. The woman is not property. She is a person. Nor is she merely a sexual object. She is not even a fragile object. She is the equal of the man as a person.

As mates, husband and wife communicate at the personal level. This includes the communication of sexual intercourse, but it also includes more. Husband and wife are companions. Their physical mating is inseparable from their mating as persons.

Sexual communication does not exist by itself

in the one flesh relationship. It is not meant to replace other forms of communication, especially the basic form of using words to talk together. In fact, the enjoyment of sexual intimacy itself is heightened when it is accompanied by words. The sharing of thoughts, feelings, wishes, and needs through words is vital to an intimate relationship.

Your talking together about yourselves, your interests, and concerns before marriage continues in marriage and hopefully will increase.

READ MARK 10:1-16

We are grateful, Lord, for the institution of marriage and specifically for our marriage. Grant that we may grow in our relationship of one flesh as we share our hearts and lives together, through Jesus Christ our Lord. Amen

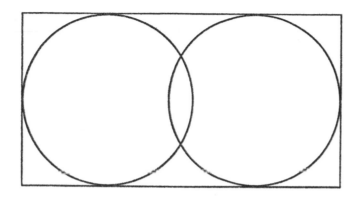

MALE AND FEMALE
HE MADE US

The one flesh relationship is not simply the joining of two persons. It is the joining of two persons who are male and female. "From the beginning of creation, God made them male and female," with a built-in attraction for each other.

This attraction brought you two together. Recall how you first met, what thoughts and feelings each of you had toward the other on that occasion, and what changes in these thoughts and feelings developed as your acquaintance increased. Like positive and negative ions, male and female are drawn to one another.

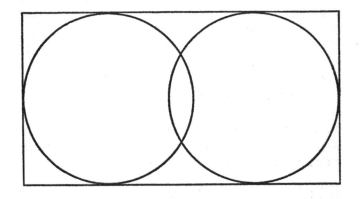

AN INNER DIALOG

To what other relationship could you compare your marriage? You might compare it to a friendship or to living with a roommate. Yet you know how different these relationships are from what you now have with your mate. In strictly human categories, it is difficult to find a comparable relationship. From ancient times, however, the marital relationship has been compared to the relationship of God to his people.

Religion is essentially a relationship. Paul Tournier calls it "the inner dialog." All religious rituals, doctrines, customs, and ethics stem from this relationship and are based on it.

A relationship exists between persons. The religious relationship is an inner dialog with God, whom we know in a personal way. When we use the pronoun for God we say "he." Yet we know that "he" is not a male in the biological sense of the term. God encompasses all personal characteristics, including those we may associate with femininity.

Depicting God as masculine may hinder our relationship with him, particularly if our image of masculine is a cultural stereotype. The imbalance may lead to compensations such as the exaltation of the Virgin Mary to fulfill the feminine balance. The church father Irenaeus thought of Mary as the new Eve, even as St. Paul called Christ the second Adam. Adam and Eve formed the initial marriage in the Garden of Eden, the one flesh relationship in which a man cleaves to a woman.

In the Old and New Testaments this symbol of one flesh is used to describe God's relationship with his people. The worshiping community is compared to a spouse. The female church is the "bride adorned for her husband," as described in the Book of Revelation.

God and his people form a one flesh relationship described in the New Testament as a relationship between Christ and his church. In belonging to the people of God, you have been involved already in a one flesh relationship. Spiritually speaking, you have already experienced a marriage before you were married. This prior experience will influence your experience with your mate. The inner dialog with God has a direct bearing on married life.

In our inner dialog with God whatever sensory symbols of communication we use are for our own needs. With our mate we experience an outer dialog in which sensory symbols such as words are used in meeting both our needs. Yet communication in marital intimacy may seem at times also to be an inner dialog when the use of words seems unnecessary.

Both the marriage of Christ and his church and that of a man and a woman have community dimensions. The church is by its very nature a community. Yet it reaches out to the larger community of human society. Your marriage likewise exists in the midst of a community of interdependent persons in which it forms a unit.

What does your personal relationship to God, and to the people of God, mean to you? I ask this question not to make you feel guilty or even inadequate, but simply to assist you in recognizing the connection between your religious life and your marriage. The marital relationship is not sufficient in itself, even though it is an entity in itself. Your one flesh relationship needs also to reach out to others for its own development.

The church is a good opportunity to experience this wider fellowship. Not only are you likely to find friends in a local congregation, but the fellowship it offers is connected with your marriage relationship to God.

Not that your wider involvement should confine

itself to the church. The people of God do not withdraw into themselves, but involve themselves with others in the world. Reach out as a couple to a wide range of people who may be open to your friendship.

READ EPHESIANS 5:21-33

Since we give as we have received, open us, Lord, to receive from you the love that comes through Christ to his church, so that we may give this love to one another as husband and wife, and to others as friends and neighbors, through the same Jesus Christ, our Lord. Amen.

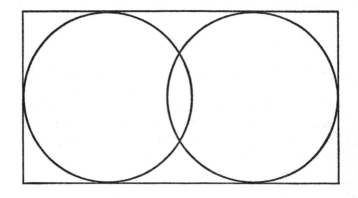

PRAYING TOGETHER

When the disciple Peter saw Jesus coming to him on the water, he wanted to try walking on the water. When Jesus told him to come, he moved to the side of the boat. As he stepped out, he lost his nerve. He began to sink and cried out to Jesus, "Lord, save me!"

This cry is a universal form of prayer. A noted newsman said that as a rational person he resorted to prayer only when his back was against the wall. When he prayed for help under these conditions, he felt miserably guilty. Resorting to prayer only when his own resources for coping were exhausted, he felt embarrassed that he was using God only for his emergencies.

The newsman viewed his feeling of guilt as an uncomfortable tension that would pass as soon as he could go it on his own again. Guilt has a purpose. It is a judgment on our behavior. It is a stimulus, therefore, to change our behavior. The newsman could have taken his cue from his discomfort and enlarged his prayer life. If one engages in the inner dialog only in periods of great stress, his relationship to God may remain as undeveloped as his prayer life.

To reserve prayer for times of great stress is a primitive though genuine religious tendency. Stress prayers are genuine because the petitioner is sincerely expressing his need. They are also primitive because they constitute the beginnings of the relationship rather than its development. As an inner dialog, prayer is sharing one's self with God. This means communicating not only our stresses but also our joys or even our boredom.

As participation in a sharing relationship, the inner dialog is a way of realizing the presence of God. The act of praying does not usher in the presence of God. Rather it indicates our awareness of this presence. Actually prayer is our response to this awareness. Yet the act of praying may also expand our consciousness of his presence.

After his resurrection Jesus said to his followers, "Lo, I am with you always." The inner dialog has an aura of privacy about it. Our awareness of God's presence comes through what William James called "the inner door of consciousness." Jesus said, "When you pray, go into your room and shut the door and pray to your Father who is in secret." This was said in reaction to the Pharisees' practice of praying ostentatiously in public. Jesus' emphasis is on the privacy of prayer.

You will want to continue your privacy in prayer even though you are married. Prayer is one of those dimensions of individuality that marital partners need to maintain as an individual activity. If your personal prayer life could stand improvement, now is the time to vitalize it, to pray to the Father in secret.

But this is only half of the story. Your need also is to join together, husband and wife, in prayer. In praying together you are expressing your new one flesh relationship before God. This new creation, your new creation, your togetherness, is being put into action. Jesus said, "Where two or three are gathered together in my name, there am I in the midst of them." Gathered together in prayer you are the church in its one flesh relationship with God.

READ LUKE 11:1-13

Grant us, O Lord, to pass this day in gladness and peace, without stumbling and stain, that reaching the eventide victorious over all temptation through your ever present aid, we may praise you, the only true God, who governs all things, through Jesus Christ, our Lord. Amen.

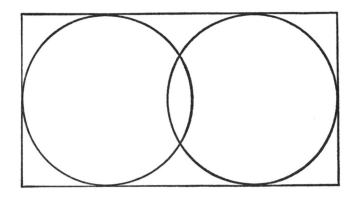

AN OPEN DIALOG

An openness to God in the inner dialog has its other side in an openness to our mate in the outer dialog. As the most intimate of human relationships, the marital union is charged with feelings. These feelings are positive. Your attraction to one another feels good. You have enjoyed good feelings in being together, doing things together, making love together.

There are also negative feelings. How do you cope with them? This is the important question. Irritations and other tensions are inevitable between marital partners simply because of the closeness of their relationship and the intensity of their care for each other.

You have probably had your share of negative feelings in your relationship. You can probably recall quite well those times when you were irritated or hurt by the other's seemingly inconsiderate behavior. How did you manage your irritation, your hurt? Your answer is important because there will be other such incidents in the future.

When we have negative feelings, we manifest them in one way or another. The important question is whether these feelings are expressed in ways that assist communication or obstruct it.

Some persons withdraw when they feel negative. Joe is an example. When he is irritated, he becomes quiet. Noticing his withdrawal his wife asks him what is wrong. "Nothing," he says. For the next hour or so he talks only when necessary. He leaves his wife no way to come to grips with what she may have said or done to offend him.

In contrast, others lash out with such intensity when they feel negative that their openness becomes destructive. Betty is an example of this. When she blows, she really blows. This in itself would be all right except that when it happens she becomes so angry that her husband also is left with little he can do. Everything he says brings on an irrational outburst until he also becomes destructive in a counterattack on her.

Evidently there is more than meets the eye in Betty's outbursts. She seems to need this kind of destructive binge as an outlet for her pent-up hostility. Consequently she resists the evident purpose of a marital quarrel, which is to penetrate whatever blocks have developed to communication. Instead she exploits the opportunity by her violent irrationality. If the purpose for expressing negative feelings is to facilitate communication, neither Joe nor Betty are expressing these feelings toward this end.

What are your patterns for expressing negative feelings—as individuals, as a couple? Does one of you tend to hold them in? Is one of you likely to flare up with little warning? Do you keep silent about your hurts and grievances? Or do you explode and then discover you are over it? Perhaps instead you let them out indirectly by needling the other with criticism and digs. Are you matched with your partner in these characteristics, or are you different?

The answers to these questions ought to reveal the situation you must take into account in developing your marital relationship. Here are a few suggestions. First, let your feelings out directly. Second, agree to work through these feelings together. As difficult as it is, listen to the other. As difficult as it is, attempt to feel with the other, to see things from his or her point of view. This is not a way of capitulating but of understanding how the other feels. In so doing you will counteract your tendency—shared by all of us—to be wholly self-centered in your quarrels, listening and feeling only with yourself.

When negative feelings are expressed and accepted, positive feelings are also expressed. When you experience positive feelings, identify them to yourself and express them also to your mate.

Because of their background some persons have as much difficulty expressing their positive feelings as others do with their negative feelings. They either feel embarrassed, or fear that they may foster too much pride in the other, or may give the other an advantage over them. In holding back their positive expressions they are failing to use the most direct way of showing their love. Their marital intimacy needs opportunities for each to express his feelings to the other, positive and negative.

The writer of the 77th Psalm had this kind of openness in his relationship to God. Note how he expresses both his negative and positive feelings in this dialog with God.

READ PSALM 77

As you have established openness in our relationship with you, Father, through the life, death, and resurrection of your Son, Jesus Christ, help us to establish this same openness in our relationship with one another, that we may know the closeness available to us in our marriage, through the same, Jesus Christ, our Lord. Amen.

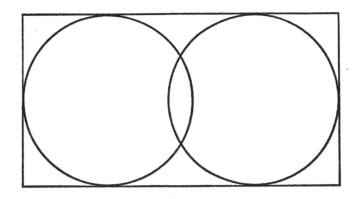

CARING
FOR FEELINGS

It would be too simple a definition of marital openness to say that all feelings one partner has should be expressed in words to the other. It would be too simple because we human beings are not that simple. Only too clearly we see—at least in retrospect—how in certain situations we color the issues. We realize we are not being rational, fair, or objective in our momentary surge of emotion.

The practice of scapegoating offers one example. In your previous family relationship or even in your relationship with one another before marriage, you may have used another person as a convenient outlet for frustrations oriented else-where. You had a need to lash out at somebody, and a family intimate—especially a mate—makes an easy target. He is available—you can get at him; and he is committed—he will "take" it. In contrast the actual targets of our frustration are often neither available nor committed to us. So it is an easy out to exploit the substitute, even though we love him.

Rather than become addicted to the practice of scapegoating those whom we love, it is better to withdraw to another room and give a soft chair a good kick or two. Perhaps also we can become as children and slap a teddy bear around. In play therapy children with pent up anger are permitted to stick pins in dollies who represent mother, father, or baby sister. We have long recognized the value of sports, athletics, and other games as harmless outlets for hostilities that need to be released.

Playing a role is another example of a distorted openness. Suppose you know from previous ex-perience that if you say a specific something to your mate under certain circumstances, he will respond in an irritating way. Yet you say it any-way and then become angry when he reacts as you anticipated. Why should we permit ourselves to play these roles under the guise of innocence?

Marriage is a dynamic stimulus–response rela-tionship. Because you are one flesh, there is little that either of you do or say that does not affect the other in one way or another. The stimulus you provide to your mate, therefore, ought to be the kind that brings forth the response you desire.

Is it? It is a good exercise in basic honesty to scrutinize the stimuli you are providing to see whether they are the kind that bring the response you supposedly desire.

The husband, for example, who says he criticizes his wife in her driving to make her a better driver, probably realizes that his criticisms make her nervous and therefore a poorer driver. What kind of a response does he really want? His knowledge of human nature ought to be sufficient to show him that he is either stupid or of two minds in the kind of stimuli he is giving his wife.

Our problem is that we don't function according to our knowledge of human nature as much as according to habit patterns that we have built up over the years. We play the same roles, provide the same perverse stimuli, and respond in the expected way because we know the "script" by heart. Eric Berne sees these as "scripts" to games we play. Because they are games, they obstruct the kind of honest relating needed for intimacy.

Berne describes several games played particularly by married couples. An example of these is the game he calls "Corner." The idea of the game is to provoke the other into saying something he doesn't mean, and then to take him up on it. As the two prepare to go to a movie, for instance, one may bring up something he knows is a bone of contention. When he gets the expected irritated reaction he may say, "If that's the way you feel, you can go to the movie yourself!" The other immediately takes him up on it. "Okay, I will!"

She says this, however, knowing he really did not want to be taken seriously. But she has him cornered and can't resist the temptation to make him eat his words.

Openness is not the same as an automatic expression of all feelings. As human beings we have the potential to manage our feelings rather than being managed by them. We are endowed with the ability to make decisions. The control system by which we make and carry out these decisions obviously needs an intelligent basis of operation. This basis includes our reason and whatever intuitive understanding we accumulate from the wisdom of experience.

These sources for management need to be utilized in your relationship with one another. There are times when you should express your negative feelings. There are other times when your obvious perverseness should give you the clue to hold your tongue. The tongue needs discipline like any other human organ that is under our voluntary nervous system.

When we use our reason along with our feelings, we are in a better position to relate with our total person, exercising the capacities we have as human beings.

READ JAMES 3

O Lord, give us discipline in the management of our feelings, that we may be delivered from the tendency to abuse those whom we love and who love us, through Jesus Christ, who loved us and gave himself for us. Amen.

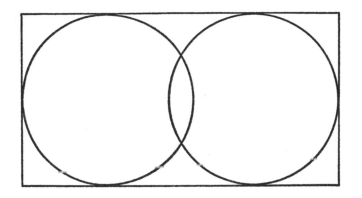

ACCEPTANCE
AND
RECONCILIATION

Your relationship needs something solid, a foundation, on which it can build. Naturally your relationship itself is its own foundation, but I am referring to the quality of this relationship. You need the kind of relationship that can tolerate openness of expression and can also be a stimulus for the achievement of discipline. This quality—this basis for relationship—is the acceptance of oneself and one's mate as he or she is. When we can accept, or take, each as he is, we are predisposed to reconciliation whenever tensions and misunderstandings disrupt the relationship. In turn, the experience of reconciliation permits these tensions and misunderstandings to be used as growth experiences in your marriage.

The picture of marriage to express the relationship between Christ and his church is helpful. The inner dialog is made possible through an inner security, acceptance with God. We can share ourselves with him because we believe we are accepted by him as we are. We are loved *from within*.

No marriage between husband and wife can take the place of the marriage with Christ any more than a mate can take the place of God. When we demand more of marriage or of a mate than either can possibly fulfill, we are doomed to disillusion. Making gods out of persons is harmful to both parties.

Your marital relationship will continue to grow because it is undergirded by the acceptance you experience in your relationship with God and with one another. Without the security of this acceptance we tend to interpret any openness in negative feelings as a personal attack equal to rejection. When we feel rejected, we either lash out in a bitter counterattack or withdraw into apathy within ourselves.

You may be wondering how much of this acceptance you have. Most of us could stand more of it. In fact, the lack of this acceptance is one way of describing the human predicament. It was to deal with this predicament that God entered the human scene in the person of his son, the man Jesus. His purpose was to communicate through his words and acts this acceptance of God. The

Good News is that God's love is unconditional. He loves you.

It takes more than words to make something effective. This is why prayer and worship and human relationships are important. They provide us the experiences with God and his people that make the words about acceptance meaningful.

We have been stressing the influence of our relationship with God on our human relationships. Actually this is a two-way street. Jesus Christ has come in the flesh. This means he participated as a human being in the human situation. We continue to know him in the flesh, that is, through our human relationships with his people. Our relationship with people influences our relationship with God.

1719541

This is especially true in marriage. As the human analogy to the relationship with the divine, the intimacy of the one flesh relationship has the potential for revealing the unconditional love of God. Your marriage is no exception. God can communicate his acceptance to your mate through you. You can receive God's acceptance of you through your mate. Through the intimacy of your love together, you can know and experience the love of God.

This mutuality between our inner dialog with Christ and our outer dialog with our mate comes to a focus in the act of reconciliation. As you use words in prayer when you feel the weight of guilt and experience the forgiveness of God, so also you can use words with your mate to experience reconciliation in the aftermath of a tiff. In this moment of reconciliation both relationships, human and divine, feed into each other.

When your relationship is strained by a flare-up of negative feelings and you feel bad about it, don't waste any time or coddle any pride. Make the overture for reconciliation with God and with your mate.

The prophet Hosea had his troubles with marriage. Like others he probably gained insights through these experiences. His advice to "take with you words and return to the Lord" probably came out of the fires of his own experiences.

READ HOSEA 14:1-7

O God, more willing to give than we are able to receive, you have shown us that in Jesus Christ you have reconciled us to you. Overcome, we pray, our stubborn resistance to reconciliation in any particular moment, so that receiving your forgiveness, we may be able to give and receive forgiveness in our marriage, through Jesus Christ, our Redeemer. Amen.

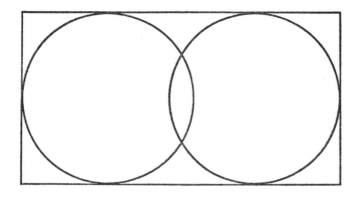

BUILDING UP
ONE ANOTHER

Have you noticed the testimonials people receive
when they die? Immediate acquaintances are
quick to say something positive. What would a
deceased person think if he could hear these
plaudits? He might say, "How ironical that I hear
such things when I'm dead!" The irony, of course,
is that he hears nothing, and that he could have
benefited from kind words in his lifetime.

This practice of reserving our praises for the
dead, or for someone's retirement ceremony, is
another indication of how blocked we are in expressing our positive feelings and appreciation
to others. Some of those who praise the dead, of

course, may be attempting to atone. Even so, what are they atoning for, except for the failure to be positive when they had the opportunity? They have a need to balance the record, but their efforts are after the fact.

We in the human family need support from one another to stimulate our self-esteem. Each is more shaky and fragile than others realize. Most of us are vulnerable when it comes to self-confidence. We need the respect and appreciation of others. Consequently we should use whatever influence we have with another to build him up rather than to tear him down. In writing to his Corinthian congregation about whom he was hearing disturbing reports, St. Paul describes his authority over them as given by the Lord for "building you up and not for tearing you down," and voices the hope that when he comes in person he will use it in this manner.

To be realized, this support needs to be communicated tangibly. The wife likes to hear her husband say, "I love you." One might argue that she ought to know that already, but such an argument misses the point. We may know many things, but we need reassurance. Knowing in these areas is like faith; it is subject to doubt. So tell me again—and again, "I love you."

The husband likes to hear his wife say, "You are my man whom I appreciate and respect." Supposedly he knows this, but his male ego has its ups and downs, and he needs reassurance.

Some rely on criticism to do the job. By pointing out where the other is deficient, they believe they are building him up. Of course, there are times when we need to receive precisely this kind of negative confrontation. There are times when we need to give it as well. Supporting one another does not mean indulging the other or protecting the other from facing the truth. Yet a steady diet of criticism tends to tear down rather than to build up.

People who criticize repeatedly are playing a game called, "I'm Only Trying to Help." Though they say this, they are not really helping. If they wanted to help, they would go about it in a different way. They have a need to criticize, and they need a victim. The game would be over if their criticism actually helped. If the criticism were at all objective, the critic would take cognizance of the person's strong points as well as his deficiencies. Because he doesn't, his criticism appears as an attack on the other. At least it has the effect of undermining the other's confidence.

We can take criticism much better and with more profit when we also receive some praise. We need appreciation to sustain our morale. It feels good to hear that someone about whom we care values what we do, or say, or what we mean to him as a person. When you like what the other has done, tell him. When you are impressed by how nice she looks, tell her. When you realize how much he means to you, tell him. When you appreciate what a fine person she is, tell her. If he handled the situation well, tell him. If her ideas are good, give her credit.

If support is offered, it needs also to be received. In order for you to give, the other needs to be open to receive. For the other to give, you need to be open to receive. Some find receiving support more difficult than giving support. When they receive a compliment, they disparage it. They turn away from praise, making the giver feel uncomfortable. When you are offered support, accept it graciously.

Rather than sparing the other the hard realities of life, a supportive relationship is one that inspires the other to accept these realities. It is an encouragement to affirm himself in his own capabilities. When someone else believes in you, particularly your man or your woman, it is easier to believe in yourself.

READ 1 CORINTHIANS 13

Help us, Lord, to believe in our own worth, and to be sensitive to the need of others to believe also in their worth, in the name of Jesus who lives to make intercession for us. Amen.

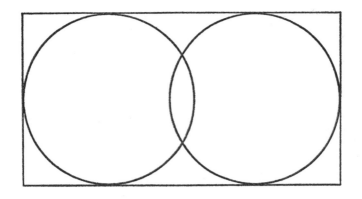

MOVING
TOWARD INTIMACY

The games people play in their intimate relationships would not be obstructive to intimacy if they were actually games. When they are confused with serious communication, they are no longer forms of entertainment, though they are stimulating. Instead they are substitutes for a vital element in relationships—intimacy.

Intimacy is the alternative to games. Games are played to avoid intimacy. The roles assumed prevent the persons from moving toward one another. Concealing the person who plays them, these roles come between the persons involved.

41

Take, for example, the game, "I'm Only Trying to Help." The very fact that one would say, "I'm only trying to help," indicates his help is not being appreciated. Why not? Let him ask the one whom he is supposedly trying to help. The answer he gets is likely to be quite direct. If he accepts the answer, he would presumably change his behavior.

Unfortunately the procedure is usually not this simple. It takes at least two persons to play a game. The one who is supposedly being "helped" is also a player. He is cooperating with the game even though he doesn't recognize it and even protests it. Each player, therefore, is supporting the other. If one refuses to play in a two-handed game, the game is over.

For a game to cease, at least one of the players must be willing to change his behavior. To be willing to make his change means that he is open to intimacy. This takes a certain amount of courage, for intimacy is not as protected by roles and boundaries as is the game. There is a risk in intimate involvement, for intimacy centers in the mystery of love. No one knows for sure where love will take him once he begins acting on it.

How shall we define intimacy? It is a quality of a loving relationship, of course. Yet it has two major characteristics, genuineness and affection. The sharing that takes place reveals rather than conceals the persons involved. The affection they feel moves them toward one another. They desire to touch, to experience physically the attraction they feel.

The language we use to express how it feels to be intimate is related to our early images of security. We feel warm, comfortable, good. "I feel close to you." Perhaps you have said this to one another. In feeling close, you feel "felt with," understood, loved as you are, "from the inside." These feelings are opposite those associated with distance, alienation, isolation—with erecting a facade. The warmth and openness of intimacy is the enjoyment of being friends, of knowing another person and of being known.

The analogy again is with religious intimacy. When St. Paul wrote to the Galatians, "Now that you have come to know God," he immediately qualified his statement by saying, "or rather to be known by God." He expanded on this mutuality of knowing in his familiar thirteenth chapter of 1 Corinthians: "Now I know in part; then I shall understand fully, even as I have been fully understood."

To Paul it is the spirit of the person who communicates the person. "For what person knows a man's thoughts except the spirit of the man which is in him? So also no one comprehends the thoughts of God except the Spirit of God." In the eighth chapter of Romans he climaxes his description of religious intimacy. "When we cry, 'Abba! Father!' it is the Spirit himself bearing witness with our spirit that we are children of God, and if children, then heirs, heirs of God and fellow heirs with Christ."

By revealing himself, God has joined himself to us. The analogy to the physical touch is the sacrament of Holy Communion. The physical suste-

43

nance of food and drink are tangible forms of communication.

But intimacy also includes tensions. If we are open to these tensions and the negative feelings involved, we are rewarded by the positive side of intimacy. If we evade these tensions to have peace, the peace we get is peace without intimacy.

In marriage the intimacy of words is supplemented by the intimacy of touch. There is body contact, tender, loving, passionate. The spoken words and the body contact are of one piece in the one flesh relationship.

The comparison is again to the Holy Communion. Here the words of Scripture are important, but they are accompanied by the bread and the cup. Intimacy is experienced through taste as well as by hearing and seeing. Eating and drinking are symbols of taking in, internalizing, the Lord, his Spirit bearing witness with our spirit.

READ ROMANS 8

O Lord, help us to accept the pain and strife that accompany our family intimacies, so that we may also experience the warmth and security inherent in all intimacy. Amen.

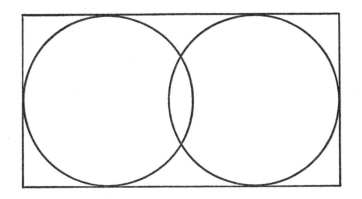

"NOW ADAM
KNEW HIS WIFE"

The intimate touch takes on added dimensions in the male–female attraction. The entire range of these dimensions is covered by what is surely the most popular of words—sex. In your relationship, too, sex occupies an important place, probably a very pleasant one. Possibly, however, it may be causing you some problems. In either case you know what it is to have desire for the other, to feel physically stimulated by the sight and the touch of the other. Sex was a factor, probably a major factor, in your decision to marry.

Now that you are married, sex continues to be a focal point of your attraction. No human experience is more full of feelings than sexual intercourse. So intense is the emotion that we use a word originally associated with suffering and agony to describe it—passion. The empathy of the lovers with one another finds a tangible expression. They feel in—into one another. They join, unite physically, become one flesh. The male enters the female; the female takes in the male. They explode, sometimes together, sometimes apart, in euphoria, elation, ecstasy, in excruciating pleasure. The act is a celebration of the union. It is a spree, an emotional binge. Yet it has a structure. What appears to be an abandon to desire is buttressed by commitment. The feelings can be turned loose in delight because the relationship is secure enough to contain them.

The word used in both Old and New Testaments to denote sexual intimacy is *know*. "Now Adam knew Eve his wife, and she conceived, and bore Cain." Know is a very personal word, meaning in this instance, to know a person. The word intimacy means literally "in the innermost." To know another is to penetrate the external coverings to her innermost, her person. Sexual intercourse is an obvious symbol of this penetration. The joining of male and female bodies forms a union symbolic of marriage.

Yet the experience of sexual intercourse can be separated from the experience of knowing. Here commitment makes the difference. When the man and woman are committed to one another, the symbol is genuine. Their sexual intercourse constitutes the body's adaptation to the pleasures of intimacy. The physical nature adds its own dimensions of delight to those of the spirit. This pleasure is present, of course, even when there is no commitment. This is why sex has such universal attraction. Yet this pleasure rarely continues in a long-term relationship without commitment. Where commitment is lacking, the novelty of change in partners may be needed to perpetuate the pleasure.

By definition a committed relationship, marriage has the potential for not only perpetuating but also for expanding the pleasures of sexual intimacy. In marriage the sexual lot is cast with the relationship. Sexual intimacy is an expression of the intimate relationship. Each feeds into the other. As the relationship deepens, its sexual expression should also deepen; and as the sexual intimacy becomes increasingly satisfying, the relationship is the direct beneficiary.

If you are not yet where you want to be as a couple sexually, you have everything in your favor to move in this direction. If you are finding your sexual intimacy satisfying, you can anticipate even more satisfaction as your relationship continues to develop.

Your commitment gives a context of meaning to your sexual experience that would otherwise be missing. In your sexual intimacy you are celebrating a relationship that unites the dimensions of time. Your relationship has a history, a past which has led you to where you are now, in the present. The experience of sexual pleasure is itself an involvement in the present. Because you are committed, your relationship has a future to which you are joined by your hopes and anticipations as a couple.

Your commitment to one another places the sexual experience within the context of God and your marital relationship to him. Within this context you can abandon yourselves to enjoyment. Rather than being an escapist tangent, your abandonment to your passions is within the mainstream of your life. It is an ecstacy in harmony with the most serious dimensions of existence. In your sex life you are participating in the joy of creation, of life, of love, of God.

The difference between a committed and an uncommitted involvement in sex was an important issue in the early church. The New Testament letters frequently refer to it. The letter to the Hebrews contains a simple description of the difference and of the consequences.

READ HEBREWS 13:1-6

We thank you, Father, for the enjoyment of sex, and ask that in our repeated celebrations of our union in this intimate way, we may continue to direct our gratitude to you, through Christ, our Lord. Amen.

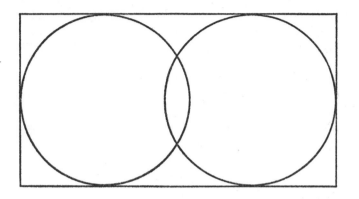

SEXUAL
SENSITIVITY

The sexual dimensions of the human psyche are highly charged. They are packed with emotions. Our feelings in the sexual area are obviously those of desire. But they may be also those of hurt and humiliation, of anger and frustration, even of repulsion.

A wife with such negative sensitivities said, "It's always got to be when he wants it, whether I feel like it or not. But it's a different story when I want it. Then he says I'm not being feminine." The husband, as we might expect, sees it differently. Usually we interpret these situations in terms of our own hurts. "I don't know how she can be so insensitive," he said. "She knows how I feel, but she doesn't seem to care. I honestly think that just knowing I want her makes her 'too tired.' " For others the situation is reversed. It is the woman who feels deprived by a husband who seems to have grown sexually indifferent.

In either case we face the question, "Whose fault is it?" Is it the one who seems indifferent to the overtures of the other, or the one who makes an overture in the face of the other's disinterest? The truth is that both are lacking in sensitivity. One is simply aggravating the other. The challenge to all marital partners is to develop an awareness of the sexual sensitivities of the other.

What are some of the things that turn off a partner sexually? Number one is probably critical conversation. If a mate makes critical remarks to the other, regardless of how subtle or indirect, he is diminishing her desire for him. These remarks may pertain to her appearance or her behavior—it matters little. The consequence is the same: the ardor is cooled.

Irritating habits are common obstacles to sexual communication. Some have a very unsubtle approach to affection. They are so preoccupied with their own needs that they seek their satisfaction at the expense of the satisfaction of the other. Their own needs get in the way of meeting the needs of their partner.

Carelessness in appearance or in bodily hygiene is another way to curtail desire. Most of us are highly sensitive to odors. Men in particular are sensitive to visual stimuli. Few persons deliberately let themselves become physically offensive. Carelessness seems to creep up on them. They may not realize that their carelessness is a form of insensitivity to the needs of their partner. But it is.

In contrast, what turns one on sexually? Positive conversation is probably number one. Using words to build the other up, expressing appreciation for the person as well as the body of the other, whets the sexual appetite. Obviously such affirmations of the other's value should be sincere, otherwise they are discerned as manipulatory and resented.

Positive habit patterns are probably second. When our sensitivity to the other is functioning, we tend to develop ways of approach that create anticipation. Women in particular appreciate affection at other times as well as for sexual stimulation. Appearance is another form of positive stimulation. Though we differ to some extent in what appeals to us, marital partners are in a position to perceive what is attractive to the other.

Through this exercise of their sexual sensitivity marital partners can assist one another in creating an anticipation for the intimate celebration of their union. As your relationship grows, you develop communication signals, more hidden than open, that subtly reveal your interest. In these preparatory ways you contribute to the other's excitement.

Subtlety enhances desire. Its innuendos and double meanings become the occasion for the build-up of anticipation. Use your creative imagination, poetic nature, and playful disposition to add variety to your approach.

Sexual sensitivity is a form of sensitivity. It amounts to being sensitive to the relationship as a whole. In the stimulus-response dynamic of one flesh, signals are being given, openly and subtly, and hopefully are being received. Sexual sensitivity and sensitivity to the relationship are related because it is the relationship that is expressed sexually. Sensitivity, then, means being aware of the feeling of your mate, and of your own.

At times we give offense to others without realizing it. We don't pick up their feelings sufficiently to know when we are saying or doing things that are "rubbing them the wrong way." This happens in marriage also. When it does, it is up to the one who is offended to make it known charitably to the other. It is then up to the offender to listen with an open mind, even though he is mystified. In this way the partners can grow in their sensitivity to the feelings of one another and in learning more effective ways of communicating these feelings.

What stimulates sexual desire? Be sensitive at this point. What brings delight to your partner? Give it. In a stimulus–response relationship you are most likely to get the response you desire by providing the stimulus the other wants.

Sensitivity is also needed in our relationship to God. St. Paul elaborates on such religious sensitivity in a prayer he includes in his letter to the Ephesians. In this prayer he uses such descriptive phrases as, "God's Spirit in our inner man," "Christ dwelling in our hearts," "power to comprehend," "knowing the love of Christ," and "filled with all the fullness of God." These all have to do with being in rapport with God. They are concerned with keeping the channels of communication open. Since sensitivity in any one intimate relationship predisposes us to be sensitive in our other relationships, the development of our religious sensitivity is mutually related to the development of our sensual sensitivity.

READ EPHESIANS 3:14-21

Father, from whom every family in heaven and on earth is named, grant us according to the riches of your glory, to be strengthened with might through your Spirit in the inner self. And grant that Christ may dwell in our hearts through faith, that being rooted and grounded in love, we may have power to comprehend with all the saints what is the breadth and length and height and depth, and to know the love of Christ which surpasses knowledge, that we may be filled with all the fullness of God. Amen.

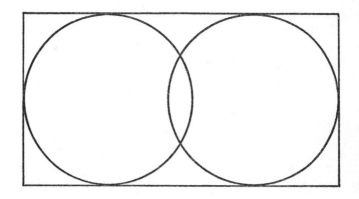

SEXUAL
FULFILLMENT

Every age is characterized by its fascination with sex. Our age, however, is super-fascinated. Kinsey's studies of human sexual habits stimulated the scientific investigation of sex. Masters and Johnson tested people as they engaged in sexual intercourse. Less scientific presentations are published in popular journals and portrayed in "adults only" films.

This stress on performance has made the sexual act more of a skill than an expression of enjoyment. Researchers say that skill is necessary for enjoyment, and to an extent this is true. Bungling is hardly conducive to ecstasy. Yet there is the greater danger of confining sex to an ego-satisfaction at the expense of a celebration of a union. Such concentration on skill predisposes one to play a role rather than to be genuine.

In this emphasis on performance other dimensions of the sexual experience may be lost. Fun, for example. It is hard to have fun in any experience in which one is pressed to measure up in performance. Overemphasis on sexual performance also endangers what the Bible calls "knowing." Sexual skill can help provide physical satisfaction; by itself it does not ensure complete personal communication.

Still another possible loss is the sacred dimension. There is more to this union than meets the eye or the testing device. A personal union has spiritual values. The mystery associated with it is not unlike that of the religious relationship. It is a "holy" experience.

Even the climax is less a climax when dominated by the performance syndrome. The peace that follows the climax comes from the security that one is loved. You lie close, and feel close, to the one who cares. The sleep that follows is rest for the spirit. One is overcome by the sheer contentment of an intimacy that has spent itself in ecstasy. This is sexual fulfillment.

As your life becomes complicated by other demands, your sexual intimacy may be neglected. The effects of such neglect are felt in feelings of separation and distance. Taking the time to make love is in the same class as taking the time to play, to enjoy life, to let go. You need it.

Otherwise an imbalance results that works against the marriage.

While there is nothing explicit in the Bible regarding sexual fulfillment, the sustaining function of sexual intimacy is implied in some advice given by St. Paul to the Corinthians. The congregation had written him concerning their questions on sex and marriage. In the seventh chapter of his letter he answers them. He clearly indicates that he favors the unmarried state. However, he specifically states that this is his opinion rather than any word from the Lord. Nevertheless, because of the sexual nature of human beings he believes it is best for people generally to be married. Christians were a tiny minority in the world of that day, and it was hard going. Paul feared that marriage would distract these few Christians from their devotion to Christ. Also he believed the second coming of Christ was imminent, so one ought to stay in whatever state he was, married or unmarried. Even if a Christian were married to a non-Christian, he is counseled to remain married.

When Paul speaks directly to married couples he gives an unequivocal word from the Lord. It is here that he shows his insight into the sexual dimensions of the one flesh relationship. "The husband should give to his wife her conjugal rights and likewise the wife to her husband." In the light of these "rights," he says, "Do not refuse one another."

There is one exception, however. If the couple wishes to devote themselves to a period of prayer, the abstinence from sex during this time would not be a violation of marital needs. Yet there are two qualifications to this exception. The couple has to make the decision *together,* and the time apart for prayer should be brief. "Then come together again, lest Satan tempt you through lack of self-control." He assumes the couple has a need for sexual intimacy and if this need were not met, it could cause problems in their marriage.

His reasoning for mutual consent on abstinence is quite simple. "For the wife does not rule over her own body, but the husband does; likewise the husband does not rule over his own body, but the wife does." Not only does he assume an equality between the sexes in this regard, but also an equal interest and desire in husband and wife for sexual intimacy. Sexual fulfillment, therefore, is the exercise of this equality and of this mutual interest in "coming together again."

READ 1 CORINTHIANS 7:1-7

Deliver us, O Lord, from the peculiar pressures of our age to perform in sex or to prove ourselves, and from all other tensions and conflicts that would deprive us of sexual enjoyment, that we may experience the full potential of this intimate union in our life together. Amen.

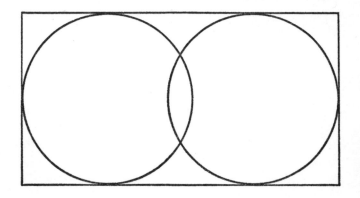

WHEN TWO
BECOME THREE

Sex as the symbol of life is also the producer of life. The marital union is a creative union; its sexual intimacy is productive of new life. Husbands and wives usually become fathers and mothers. Marriage is for companionship and for procreation, and sex has its function in both purposes. To keep one function from opposing the other, there is need for birth control measures. When these are adequate, sex for companionship is not threatened by sex for reproduction. At the same time the opportunity of sex for reproduction is available by choice. Consequently birth control measures are not only to prevent conception but also to make conception possible.

The desire of a husband and wife to become parents is not always quickly fulfilled. For some couples conception is more difficult than for others. The reasons are complex. Fortunately, competent medical assistance is available to those who desire it. There are also opportunities for adoption.

These opportunities were not always available, of course, but the resource of prayer is an age-old help. The barren woman praying for a child is a frequent theme in the Bible. The story of Hannah is typical. Her problem was aggravated because her husband, Elkanah, had another wife who not only bore him children, but tormented Hannah over her barrenness. When she became depressed Elkanah tried to comfort her. "Hannah," he said, "why do you weep? And why do you not eat? And why is your heart sad? Am I not more to you than ten sons?"

To this we can imagine Hannah saying, "Yes, but!" A husband is one thing, a child another.

In her deep distress she prayed to the Lord and vowed that if he would give her a son, she would give him to the Lord. In "due time" she conceived and bore Samuel, who became the last of the Israelite judges.

In the creation account of Genesis God speaks to man as he does to all other forms of life, "Be fruitful and multiply and fill the earth." Despite his numerous attempts to depopulate the earth through wars, man has finally succeeded in filling the earth. In fact, he has overdone it. If atomic explosion and war do not destroy us, ecologists

59

believe the population explosion will. So we have organizations such as Zero Population Growth to counteract this danger.

Yet even zero population growth means an average of two children in a marriage. Even in our day of a filled earth, married people are still needed as parents.

In the familiar description of the nuclear family husband and wife are compared to the nucleus of a molecule. They produce children who are like electrons that revolve around the nucleus. Children begin with a complete dependency on their parents. Gradually as they grow they assume more and more individual responsibility. During this long period of eighteen to twenty years they need a stable environment of sustaining relationships. They need a home. The mother and father who bring them into being are the logical ones to provide this home. When the children are mature, they leave father and mother to cleave to a mate to form another nucleus, and the process begins again.

Because you have been on only one side of the parent–child relationship, you may not be as balanced in your awareness of the parental process as you anticipate. This imbalance leads some young couples to underestimate the challenge of parenthood, or to become overconfident that they can do better than their own parents. Finding themselves on the other side of the relationship can be a sobering experience.

I do not say this to frighten you, but to emphasize the need for preparation. There is a risk in be-

coming parents, even as you took a risk when
you were married. Nobody can guarantee that
either venture will turn out as you anticipate.
There is no way to avoid risks if you want to do
anything or achieve anything. But you can mini-
mize the risks by preparatory planning, study,
and conversation with others who are involved.

There is need for continuing education in marriage and in parenthood. Take advantage of opportunities in church and community to attend
groups and classes for married couples and parents.

READ 1 SAMUEL 1

*O God, the Father of our Lord Jesus Christ and
our own Father, give us the wisdom to plan our
future together, and should we fulfill our potential for parenthood, help us to receive any child
as a gift of your love and to trust in your guid-
ance in rearing this child to maturity, through
Jesus Christ. Amen.*

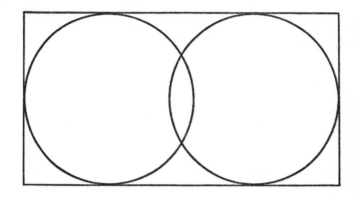

PARENTS
ARE LOVERS TOO

Even as the sexual functions in mating and in conception are not intended to work against each other, neither are the actual functions of mating and parenthood. But sometimes they do. As one husband put it who felt victimized by his wife's being a mother, "She cares about the kids more than she does about me. Frankly I feel left out."

His wife sees it differently. "Jack leaves all the responsibility for the children to me. I wish he'd help out more, but he doesn't. He's just not interested in them. So I have to do it all."

When parenthood interferes with mating, it is

not only the mates who suffer. The situation is not good for the children either. Their security centers in the security of the nucleus, the mating relationship of the parents. If they come between their parents, or are aware of trouble in the home, they become anxious or even feel guilty. On the other hand when mother and father obviously love each other, the children know that the nucleus which insures their own safety is secure.

In bringing a child to birth, marital partners are extending the scope of their partnership. Committed to one another in marriage, they take on the additional commitment to rear a child together, their child to whom they have contributed their genes. Their commitment means as much to the child as their contribution of genes. The environment they provide as parents is a significant influence in the child's maturation. Even when a child is adopted, his adoptive parents soon become his real parents because of their influence on his development.

Other adults also become involved in the child's life. They provide a supplement to the parental influence. It is helpful to parents when these other adults—relatives, teachers, neighbors, scout leaders—form relationships with the child. If these relationships become a substitute for the parents, a problem arises. Actually there can be no substitute in the child's eyes for his own father and mother so long as they are living and available. The child's identity is tied up with those whom he recognizes as his parents. If substitutes take their place when such substitutes are not a necessity, the child is likely to interpret the substitution as parental rejection. In such instances he is also likely to blame himself because his parents seem disinterested in him.

Partnership as parents implies differences in the way the two parents function. Such diversity can mean a balance in parental approach. Few of us are so complete that we would not profit from another approach or point of view. The child, therefore, ought to have a fuller experience of parenthood for having two different parents.

Differences, however, can also mean division. Few of us appreciate differences; rather we are threatened by them. We interpret differences in terms of right and wrong rather than of supplemental balance. The children then become the focus of the parents' problems in relating to one another, emotional issues in a power struggle rather than indivdiuals in their own right. Naturally parents should have some sense of unity concerning how they function with their child, but undergirding this unity is the need for the mutual respect of the other's wisdom as they talk over their partnership.

Children add to the delights and to the stresses of the couple's life together. Thus they are genuine additions to the dimensions of intimacy. During family times the functions of parenthood and marriage come together. You may recall such times in your own family life. Often they occur at mealtime or on special outings, or during holiday festivities, or on extended vacations. They are high times of enjoyment that leave pleasant memories. They can also be stress times and memorable primarily for their traumatic effect.

The home life of Jesus was no exception. The family's annual outing was the trip to Jerusalem in celebration of the Passover festival. The one recorded occasion in Jesus' childhood concerns this event. His family had joined with others in his home town of Nazareth to make the journey. All went well until they were ready to return. Jesus, then a boy of twelve years, was nowhere to be found. The others were ready to leave and his parents assumed he was with other children in the group. It was not until they had been gone a day's journey that they realized they were wrong. Alarmed, they returned alone to Jerusalem to look for him.

For three days they searched that city. Then they found him in the temple, sitting with the teachers and asking them questions. He seemed oblivious to the panic he had caused his parents. "Son, why have you treated us so?" his mother asked. But all he answered was, "How is it that you sought me? Did you not know that I must be in my father's house?"

In our times of family stress we have need for a sense of values that permits us to harmonize the mating and parental functions. Our values enable us to see more than the immediate conflict or enjoyment; rather we become aware of the dynamics in which each individual is attempting to satisfy his needs or achieve his goals. This kind of perspective comes from continuous learning through reading, reflecting on our experiences, and engaging in conversation with others.

It means also to engage in prayer for wisdom and understanding. Like King Solomon of old, we need to put such wisdom first in our petitions to God. He asked for it to govern his people; parents, no less than kings, need wisdom to rear their children. No gift is promised more to those who ask, in both Old and New Testaments, than wisdom. Says St. James, "If any of you lacks wisdom, let him ask God who gives to all men generously and without reproaching, and it will be given him. But let him ask in faith."

READ LUKE 2:41-52

O God, the protector of all that trust in you, without whom nothing is strong, nothing is holy: increase and multiply upon us your mercy; that, you being our ruler and guide, we may so pass through things temporal, that we finally lose not the things eternal; through your Son, Jesus Christ our Lord, who lives and reigns with you and the Holy Spirit, one God, ages without end. Amen.

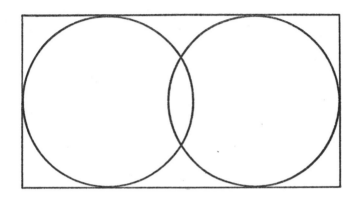

PARENTS
BUT
STILL FRIENDS

After listening to a couple describe their difficulties in marriage, the marriage counselor asked, "When was the last time you went out together?" The husband scratched his head. "I can't remember." The counselor looked at the wife. "It's been a long time," she said, "I can't remember either."

Like most other couples, their companionship was once an important part of their lives. During their courtship they dated regularly and enjoyed each other's company. Now this aspect of their relationship had all but disappeared.

What caused the decline of their companionship?

It was displaced by other activities. First they became parents. They could have balanced the parental and mating functions, but they didn't. Additional functions were also factors in preventing the balance. The husband's job took much of his time and energies. What spare time he had was taken up by a bowling league and other sporting interests. If they were to go out together, it meant hiring a baby sitter, and they hated to spend the money. So they went places separately. Gradually, without either of them realizing what was happening, their companionship was crowded out of their life.

These competing functions were all good in themselves. There is nothing anti-marriage about having a job, or participating in a bowling league, or being concerned parents. In fact each of these functions contributes to the broadening of experience. Yet by competing against marital companionship, each of them contributed to the loss of the couple's friendship.

Other functions have their set times. There is a structure, perhaps even a deadline. Companionship has none of this. It has to be "squeezed in." As a result it gets "squeezed out."

It is significant that Jesus described his relationship to his disciples by using the word *friend*. "No longer do I call you servants, for the servant does not know what his master is doing, but I have called you friends for all that I have heard of my father, I have made known unto you."

Companionship has a high priority also in our marriage to Christ. Yet here too it can get crowded out by other functions, even church work. We can exercise our friendship with Christ in any situation, but we are more likely to express it when a specific time is set aside. The practice of daily devotions is such a specific occasion. Like companionship in marriage, devotions are easily crowded out of our schedules by more "pressing" obligations. Since religion and marriage both center in knowing another, the time devoted to the presence of the other is actually of high priority to the relationship. Yet it is precisely this sort of activity in both commitments that is given low priority by our production-oriented culture.

Like other functions, companionship requires structure and the necessity for the companions to respect the structure. When we easily neglect the companionship function because of the press of other demands, we are showing where our priorities are. Our priorities in turn reveal our sense of values—what it is we deem more or less important. When companionship slips out the back door of a marriage, each partner begins to suffer from the deprivation, though involvement in other functions prevents immediate awareness of it.

In the newness of your marriages this concern over companionship may seem unrelated to you. Hopefully it is. You enjoy the other's company and do things together as companions. Your conversation is the conversation of friends. So what's the problem?

The only problem is that your companionship is a fragile thing in the competitive pressures of our cultural concerns. You will need to protect it. Continue to give your times together high priority. Prepare for your fun, think about it, let your excitement build up. Romance need never leave your marriage, for romance centers in your attitude toward priorities. When you make plans, you build your anticipation, providing you know you can count on the plans. In this way you can insure the continuance of your companionship. It will become fixed in your relationship by the momentum of habit according to your determination.

READ JOHN 15:1-17

O Christ who called your disciples friends, lead us not into the temptation of sacrificing the time and energy we owe to our marriage to other demands, but deliver us from the evil of conforming to this world with its distorted values and priorities, that our friendship with you and with each other may grow day by day. Amen.

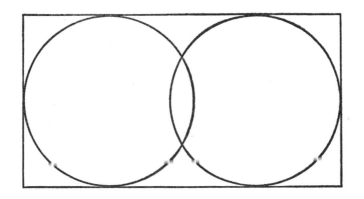

STRIKING
A BALANCE:
WORK AND FUN

As a country in which people have worked hard to "get ahead," America has been dominated by its own work ethic. This ethic implies that a man's worth is determined by his work and by his success with it. I used the word *man* instead of person because it is the man in our society who is particularly affected by this ethic. However, it is also affecting the woman, at least in how she evaluates a man. In sizing up a man as a marriage prospect or evaluating him as a marriage partner, the question of his "being a good provider" is important. "Making good money" is confused with "being a good man."

An exaggerated work ethic may take all the fun out of life and out of a marriage. Those who live to work become work addicts, and are seldom fun people. Even when they are not working, they are working at something. It may be golf, it may be bowling, but it is not fun. They are competitors, who even in games are concentrating on skills, goals, scores, progress, just as they do with their work.

In contrast, fun is aimless, imaginative, and impractical. Fun goes with play. By the very nature of play, one cannot work at it. Work has an end, a goal, while play is its own end.

Play is what children do, that is, until adults organize their play. They get lost in it, forget time, confuse facts with imagination, and follow no rules. You may be grown, but you do not cease to be a child. Your "child" helps to keep the balance with your "adult." There are occasions when the adult needs to be in charge—to be dominant. Work is an example of such an occasion. But there are other times when it is good to let your "child" be dominant. Times for fun and play are such times.

Our work ethic leads us to believe that work is more justified than play. But this is not necessarily so. Both are needed as complements for a full life. By the same token, fun is not more justified than work.

There are people who enjoy their work. They are fortunate. I hope this is your good fortune. As the Preacher in Ecclesiastes says, "It is God's gift to man that everyone should eat and drink and take pleasure in all his toil." Yet enjoying one's work is not the same as having fun. No matter how much one enjoys his work, he is dominated by goals, is pressed to finish, and gets satisfaction out of accomplishment.

Actually if you enjoy your work, you may find it even more difficult to have fun. "My husband loves his work so much," said an understanding wife, "that he would stay with it all the time. I have to remind him that there are other things in life—such as me." As enjoyable as work may be, it is not the same as the enjoyment of play. The most unpleasant of all characters in Dickens' *Christmas Carol*, Scrooge, enjoyed counting his money. In contrast, the enjoyment of play is without goals, directions, pressure, or even the desire to finish, to complete.

During your courtship the child within each of you probably had enough opportunity to take charge. Much of what goes on in dating is play. In marriage an increasing number of adult responsibilities come upon us. Marriage itself is an adult responsibility. As these responsibilities increase, your child may find it more and more difficult to have any fun. If this happens to you, your life together becomes unbalanced. The adult needs the child.

When your child cannot have his fun, he will not take it lying down. He will protest like any child when he is not getting the attention he needs. He will pout, throw temper tantrums, or get sick. Failing to get positive attention, he settles for negative attention. Anything is better than no attention.

The reaction of sickness is of particular significance. Although there are many causes for illness, an unbalanced life is one. Play is healthy. Fun is good for the body as well as for the spirit and the mind.

Another reaction to the absence of fun is excessive drinking. When fun is crowded out, the human spirit becomes dissatisfied. The recourse to drinking is a befuddled way of trying to achieve the balance. Alcohol becomes a temptation when one is either too inhibited to have fun or too driven by ambition to play.

The Preacher in Ecclesiastes says that there is "a time to plant and a time to pluck up what is planted." There is also "a time to mourn and a time to dance." "For everything," he says, "there is a season."

Dancing is the nearest to play of all the activities that the Preacher mentions. By dancing he is not referring to ballet or to any learned "step." Rather he means the kind of abandon that David manifested when he danced before the ark of God. The ark was the sacred chest used by the Israelites in their worship. It had fallen into enemy hands and had been retrieved. David as King led the procession bringing it back to the tent of worship. In doing so he cast off his royal robes and began to dance before the Lord "with all his might." His dance was the spontaneous expression of religious ecstasy. In dancing he was letting loose like a child at play. Religious ecstasy, like play, is a childlike expression of joy, of fun. In the presence of God one becomes free to play. He receives the kingdom of God as a child.

READ ECCLESIASTES 3:1-15

The ancient collect for peace, while not directly concerned about fun and work, pertains to the serenity of spirit that makes play possible:

O God, from whom all holy desires, all good counsels, and all just works do proceed: give unto your servants that peace which the world cannot give; that our hearts may be set to obey your commandments, and also that by you, we, being defended from the fear of our enemies, may pass our time in rest and quietness; through the merits of Jesus Christ our Savior, who lives and reigns with you and the Holy Spirit, one God, ages without end. Amen.

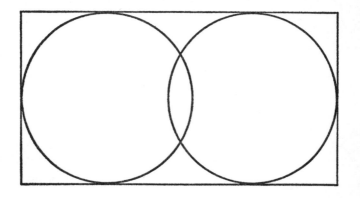

THE CROSSROADS
OF
TWO HISTORIES

Because each adult continues also to be a child, Hugh Misseldine says that four rather than two unite to form a marriage, namely the two adults and the two "inner children of the past." This foursome is active in the intimate moments of husband and wife, whether at the dinner table or in the bedroom. The two children in the foursome represent two different homes with different ways of doing things. These differences between the "children" in their past experience of family living are soon felt by the newly married adults as they attempt to merge their two lives into a unit.

Sometimes these differences in family backgrounds are in the extreme. The wife may come from a family in which none of the members displayed their emotions except in anger. In contrast the husband may come from a family in which affection was displayed openly and with gusto. What seems natural to him may seem unnatural to her.

Another contrast is in regard to anger. In the wife's family it may be common for individuals to flare up when irritated. Tempers are lost with little provocation, and after the flare-up life soon returns to normal. In the husband's family, by contrast, the members may hold their negative feelings inside themselves. Of course this cuts down on family communication. People became quiet when irritated or hurt, but there was seldom a fight. In the light of this family history how will the husband react when his wife "blows her stack"?

Another extreme may be in the attitude toward work. The wife may come from a family that lived by the American work ethic and old-fashioned thrift, while the husband may be the product of an easy-going family in which work was of secondary importance to fishing or other pastimes. What happens when the husband fails to show the drive she associates with normal behavior?

Because of differences in family histories, mates may have differing expectations of one another. If the man comes from a family in which the mother was dominant, he may expect his wife to assume responsibilities which she feels he should share. Or if he reacted against his dominant mother, he may be supersensitive to any overture that even looks like his wife is "taking over." If the wife comes from a home in which the father was dominant, she may expect her husband to be more aggressive than he actually is. Men who come from homes where "mother always did it," may expect their wives to "do it" too. So also with wives whose fathers were competent, efficient, "take charge" men. If the husband does not fit the role, he may feel in a very uncomfortable way his wife's disappointment. The one is "let down" and also disapproving, while the other is irritated but also deflated.

When we project onto a mate the patterns associated with our own family background, we are not giving him the opportunity to be who he is. If he is forced into a frame which does not fit, he will naturally resent it, and his mate will just as naturally be disappointed.

Our family history also has its influence on our own role in marriage. We tend to take on the behavior patterns of the parent of our own sex when we become emotionally upset. If your dad, for example, tended to walk away petulantly from your mother when he was provoked, as a husband you may find yourself doing this same thing when you are incensed with your wife. On the other hand if your mother broke down and cried during family arguments, as a wife you may find yourself doing the same thing. You may even say the same words.

When we consider that this is the behavior pattern you have witnessed and experienced, it is not unusual that you would simulate it under emotional stress. It is the pattern of the one with whom you were most likely to identify in your developing years and whose family role you are now fulfilling. When we have time to organize our behavior we function according to the desired image we have of ourselves, but when we are under emotional stress, we tend to talk and act out rather than to think or to plan. It is then that we are most likely to follow as if by instinct the patterns of our family background.

You are also most likely to notice this tendency in your mate before you notice it in yourself. Because you do not share your mate's family background, you observe the peculiarities of your in-laws with a sharper eye than if you were accustomed to them. When you see these same peculiarities in your spouse, you are tempted critically to point out the parallel behavior. "You are acting just like your mother!"

According to the best of marital rules, this kind of an attack on your spouse's family background is "dirty pool," not "cricket," and an obvious "no-no." Why? Because you are doing the same thing only you are not as aware of it. Like your mate you also assume uncritically that to which you have become accustomed. In attacking your spouse for being influenced by her family background, you are inviting the same kind of attack on yourself. You have initiated a mutual prejudice against differing family backgrounds which makes appreciation of these differences even more difficult.

While I may not have touched on your own differences in family histories, I am sure you have them. What are you going to do about them? These differences, are potentially enriching to your life together. They do not by necessity lead to blocks and frustrations. Utilize their potential to give fuller dimensions to your marital experience.

In marriage two individuals become one flesh. This means two family histories become one new family unit. To merge the two backgrounds does not mean that one must cancel out the other. Rather each complements the other as the basis out of which the new is created. Out of the old—in this case two olds—the new comes forth.

Your creation of a new one flesh out of two differing family nuclei will not be accomplished without tension. This tension will also be painful. How else can two individuals from distinctive backgrounds become one except by the friction —the tension—of experiencing those differences? Nor is the process accomplished once and for all. Rather it is continuous. Our marriage is always in the process of becoming. Growth and development are the characteristics of a healthy marriage regardless of its age. This mutual enterprise of husband and wife has as its greatest asset the openness of each to that with which he or she is not accustomed. Let there be no assumed superiority of one family background in contrast to the other, and thus no assumed inferiority.

The spirit of openness that makes for this kind of genuine appreciation for difference is the opposite to the attitude of judgment described by St. Paul in the second chapter of Romans. Do you not know, you who judge your brother, neighbor, spouse, that you do the same things? Your judgmental attitude closes your mind to your own involvement in the very fault that you are finding in your mate.

READ ROMANS 2:1-4

Reveal to us, Lord, an understanding of ourselves that we may be aware of what is happening when our predispositions are obstructing our acceptance of others, and liberate us from bondage to these arbitrary judgments, that we may grow to appreciate the uniqueness of each individual. Amen.

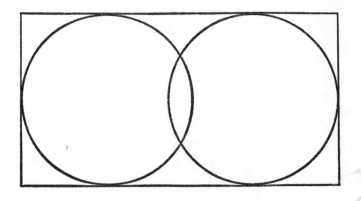

HARMONY
WITH IN-LAWS

The living embodiment of the two different life histories that are merging in your marriage are your two sets of parents. Your in-laws are people to get to know better. They are your family now. You have been accustomed to your own family circle, but when you married that circle became much wider. This is a reality you need inwardly to accept. Open up to your new in-laws and take them in.

Taking them into your family circle is not the same as taking them into your marriage. Your marriage belongs to the two of you. It can only be weakened if your parents and in-laws enter into the nucleus. This can happen if your relationship to them is poorly structured. When in-laws are accused of interference, the difficulties usually stem from the beginning of the marriage. Though only minor irritations then, later they became major sore spots because they were not dealt with directly, but were permitted to pile up.

Your relationship with your own parents changes when you become one flesh with another. Your mate now shares in your parental relationships. They have become his or her in-laws. Your mate, therefore, should not be put into the position of feeling excluded from your relationship to your parents. If you and your parents have private conversations in one room while your mate sits isolated in another, he will probably resent it, although he says nothing at the moment. The same isolation may take place if the conversation that takes place is always oriented to your family's interests, acquaintances, and past history.

Your parents need reassurance concerning their relationship to you. The change from you-as-their-child to you-as-married-to-another may be difficult for them. If you are their first child to be married, it may be all the more difficult. Much depends also on the role you had in their lives and in the life of the family.

Some of the reassurance they need can be given verbally. Parents like to hear that they are still loved and appreciated. Reassurance can also be given by the little considerations you give to their feelings. Being considerate, however, is not the same as making concessions that are against the best interests of your marriage. You have left father and mother to cleave to a mate. The order of loyalties is clear.

In fact, leaving father and mother is necessary for one to cleave to another. Yet the transition may be difficult for both child and parents. Such difficulties are eased by kindly consideration for feelings. In terms of the future they are also eased by your own affirmation of your adulthood. Mates who permit their parents to interfere with their marriage because they do not want to hurt them are being most unwise and unkind. Out of weakness they are putting off the needed structuring of their relationship with their parents until it will finally hurt much more. We need confidence in our parents that they can adjust to a new relationship if we hold to a structure that will ultimately benefit the relationship. Even in the immediate tension that such structuring may create, the obvious honesty in the relationship is already an asset.

Noninterference, however, is simply the absence of a negative influence. In itself it is not a positive influence. Because parents and in-laws are potential resources for a marriage, more is desired from them than noninterference. You are fortunate if you have parents and in-laws. The challenge now is to develop a positive relationship with them. Perhaps you already have a good start in this direction.

Such a positive relationship has two characteristics: the freedom to ask and the freedom to decline. Parents and in-laws have advantages that a young marriage may lack. The channels of communication should be such that you feel free to ask for help, whether for advice or even money. At the same time you need to feel the same freedom to decline the advice and to say no to offers of help, even of money. Both freedoms go together, since if one lacks the freedom to decline, he will not risk his freedom by asking.

Parents are usually quick to give advice. Therefore you need the freedom to refuse it. If it is actually freedom it means also that you are free to accept it.

As great a lawgiver and leader as Moses still was able to profit from the counsel of his father-in-law. When he had succeeded in leading the Israelites out of Egyptian slavery, they became very dependent on him. From morning until evening they brought him all of their problems, and he would intercede for them to God and offer them counsel. His father-in-law Jethro saw that such dependence would exhaust Moses' energy and time. He was too unorganized to lead effectively.

So Jethro offered a suggestion. "Listen, now to my voice," he said, "I will give you counsel." He advised Moses to choose able men and place them over a specific number of people as their counselor. Only the difficult or "great matters" would be brought to Moses. This would free Moses to concentrate on his task of leading the people. "If you do this," said Jethro, "and God so commands you, then you will be able to endure."

Moses evidently saw the wisdom in Jethro's advice. "He gave heed to the voice of his father-in-law and did all that he had said."

In spite of the fine things that can be said about parental counsel and parental support, you and your mate need also to go it alone. It won't hurt you to begin with a few deprivations. Naturally it bothers parents when they see you doing things in a way that they know from their own experience won't work. At the same time you need to learn from your own mistakes, and this means you need the freedom to make them.

Both the freedom to ask and the freedom to decline are characteristics of a positive relationship which is composed of persons who are prior to and more important than any characteristics. Parents and in-laws are people whom we can know, whom we can grow to feel good with. When you feel free, you also feel at ease. It is then that you also enjoy.

READ EXODUS 18:13-27

Our Father, help us to open our hearts to our new family, even as we ask that their hearts also may be open to us, through Jesus Christ, our Lord. Amen.

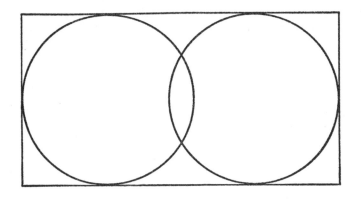

REACHING OUT
TO THE COMMUNITY

The inner circle of your family—parents, in-laws, bothers, sisters, and other close relatives—needs an outer circle of other associates. Otherwise it would only be a circle, not an inner circle. Even as your marriage is expanded by the inner circle, so also the outer circle is necessary to prevent the inner circle and your marriage from turning in on itself. Family centeredness has some of the same destructive tendencies as self-centeredness.

The outer circle includes your neighbors, your fellow workers, your mutual friends. It also includes the people in your local church.

While blood may be thicker than water, you inherit the blood but you choose the water. As the biblical proverb says, "There is a friend who sticks closer than a brother." Even as you needed friends before your marriage, so your marriage needs friends. Sometimes it is difficult for both husband and wife to develop the same feelings of attraction for the same friends. Also you may like the wife more than the husband or vice versa in any particular couple. For the sake of mutual friendships try to be open rather than critical. Perhaps you really don't know the less attractive person well enough to see any deeper than his surface behavior.

Each community has its concerns and its needs. I am sure yours is no exception. These now become your concerns and needs as you identify yourself with your community. In becoming involved in these concerns you are reaching out to the larger community, the outer circle.

There is the danger that such involvement may crowd out rather than enhance your marital companionship. The same possibility exists also in regard to your friendships. These involvements can be used as a protection against being alone as a couple. But the dangers inherent in the outer circle do not eliminate the values. Any good can be abused to the point where it becomes an evil. The outer circle has a function to fulfill for your marriage. If your marriage begins to hurt because of these involvements you are too involved, and need to ask yourself if you are possibly using your involvement as an escape from other responsibilities. As a married couple you are yourself a community in a reciprocal relationship with the larger community.

Normally your job takes you into the community and your involvement may come through it. However, when the job simply means earning a wage, the involvement may be minimal. On the other hand when you become interested in the people with whom you work and in the purpose of your work, your involvement may be significant.

The same is true with your local church. It is not simply a place to go to worship God, but rather is a gathering of a community of believers who together worship God. Involvement in your church means getting to know its people, with whom you are in fellowship. Your involvement means your sharing in the concerns and the mission of this fellowship. The local congregation is a ready-made, built-in means for reaching out to the larger circle. In fact, it is the larger circle.

Some of this outreach to the larger community will be as individuals rather than as a couple, although hopefully most of it will be as a couple. Yet even when you are involved as individuals, you can share with one another what you are doing so that in a sense you are in it together.

Priscilla and Aquila were "in it together" in all ways. They were a husband and wife team of the early church who worked together not only in the church but in their trade as tentmakers. Always they are mentioned together in the New Testament and in all but the first instance, Priscilla is mentioned first. This was unusual for the times and may indicate that Priscilla was no subdued or inferior member of a first century marriage.

St. Paul first met this remarkable couple at Corinth when he arrived there on his second missionary journey. They too had just arrived, having fled their home in Rome when the Emperor Claudius had ordered all Jews out of the capital. Since they were all of the same tentmaking trade, Paul lived with them during his stay in Corinth. When he later left for Ephesus, they accompanied him. After Paul had left them there, a young convert named Apollos arrived in Ephesus. Although eloquent in preaching the gospel, his instruction in the Christian way left something to be desired. So Priscilla and Aquila took him in hand and taught him the way of God more accurately. After this Apollos left for Corinth where he became one of the great preachers in the early Church.

Paul's affection for this couple is movingly expressed in his greeting to them in his letter to the Romans. "Greet Priscilla and Aquila, my fellow workers in Christ Jesus, who risked their lives for my life, to whom not only I but also all the churches of the Gentiles give thanks." Then he added another greeting which shows their mutual involvement in the church. "Greet also the church in their house."

From all indications Priscilla and Aquila's involvement in the larger circle of their Christian fellowship only enhanced their own marital companionship. It can do the same for yours.

READ ACTS 18

The following old collect for the Church seems fitting for this devotion:

Most gracious Father, we humbly beseech you for your holy Christian Church. Fill it with all truth, and in all truth with all peace. Where it is in error, reform it; where it is in want, furnish it; where it is right, strengthen and confirm it; and where it is rent asunder, heal the divisions thereof, through Jesus Christ our Lord. Amen.

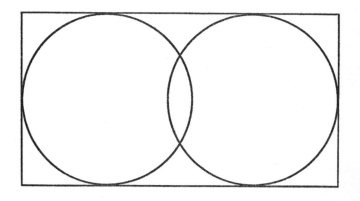

THE WORLD AROUND YOU

The mission of Christ takes us even beyond the larger community. After his resurrection the Lord said to his followers, "You shall receive power when the Holy Spirit has come upon you, and you shall be my witnesses in Jerusalem and in all Judea and Samaria and to the end of the earth." A Christian is not bound by his own neighborhood, parish, or tribe. Rather he is identified with Christ's mission of sharing the Good News of reconciliation, of healing, of hope, to the end of the earth.

The Good News is for the whole person as well as for the whole world. It influences our social, political, and economic points of view. As followers of Christ we also are persons of influence. Wherever they are, Christ's followers are concerned about reconciliation, about healing, and about hope.

Our commitment to Christ enlarges our concerns. By beginning with Jerusalem, and in all Judea and Samaria, Jesus' followers were in effect beginning at home, and from there reaching out to the larger circle of their society and community, and finally to the end of the earth. The vision is both local and global. John Wesley said, "The world is my parish." As a Christian your concern is not just your marriage, or your inner family circle, or even your community or congregation. Rather it is the whole human enterprise under God. This concern gives to your marriage a structure, a creed, an ethic, a setting.

In sharing the concern—the vision—of Christ, we desire that all people know the Good News. You can share it in your own circle of family and friends by manifesting a spirit of reconciliation, being a healing influence, and by sharing the Christian hope. You can also help others do it by supporting them financially. Your church has a home mission program, a social service program, and a world mission and service program that depend on your support.

Sharing Christ's vision means also that we are concerned that the spirit of reconciliation and justice be put into practice in our society. The prophet Micah depicts this vision in utopian terms. The days shall come when "the mountain of the house of the Lord shall be established as the highest of the mountains." Then he shall "teach us his ways," and "they shall beat their swords into plowshares, and their spears into pruning hooks; nation shall not lift up sword against nation, neither shall they learn war any more; but they shall sit every man under his vine and under his fig tree, and none shall make them afraid."

We are along way from fulfilling this vision of human life. Yet it remains our goal and our hope. We are concerned about injustices. The inequality of opportunity that exists between the white and minority races, and between the poor and the affluent is disturbing to our Christian sensitivity. What can you, your church, your local government, your local industry, do about these discrepancies?

The vision moves us to be concerned about the tendency to make war a way of life. We can't beat our spears into pruning hooks as long as we need them to kill the enemy. Everybody says he dislikes war, but not enough people really mean it. In addition to its horror, unfortunately war is also profitable. Yet it is outside the vision. Conflicts will remain, but war as the means for settling them needs more dispassionate evaluation. While decisions in these matters seem to be made in the higher echelons, in a democracy it is the people who ultimately determine how they are made.

Not only does man hurt and exploit his neighbor, he also hurts and exploits the earth. We have been poor stewards of God's air, water, and land. Yet we cannot survive without them. Again it is the people who must make their concerns felt. We show our sense of values by our priorities in our expenditures and in our efforts. These priorities, whether of a family, a community or a national government, also indicate what we are likely to achieve, or not to achieve.

It is one thing to be concerned and it is another to put our concerns into action. There are groups in most communities with whom you can join forces. The group that I believe is still the most available and effective is the church. The church is a place where people of like concerns can gather. It is also people. Christians are the church wherever they function—in government, education, health and welfare, business and industry. You are the church in your particular sphere of influence. The church is not primarily a corporation or even an organization, but a movement in which like-minded people who share the vision can think, plan, and act together in local, national, and worldwide concerns.

The local congregation is your contact with the worldwide church. It is the spot in space and time where you can tie in to the ends of the earth. There you can be influenced by the worldwide church and the worldwide church can be influenced by you.

Continue to read together, to reflect, to talk, to pray together. Use your Bible. Use books of devotion. Bring out into the open your common concerns, problems, tensions, dreams.

You have imagination. Use it in planning your

devotions. Be creative. Do things differently—but do them together.

READ MICAH 4:1-4

O Christ, fill us with the compassion that moved you to heal the sick in mind and body. Stir up our spirits in love for those who suffer from the various evils of this world. Move us to pray and to work for their deliverance, and keep us strong in the faith that all evils will ultimately be overcome by your redemptive power. Amen.